# THE
# BOOK OF
# STUPID
# QUESTIONS

# THE
# BOOK OF
# STUPID
# QUESTIONS

## TOM WELLER, PS.D.*

**WARNER BOOKS**

A Warner Communications Company

*Warner Books, Inc., 666 Fifth Avenue, New York, NY 10103*

Ⓦ A Warner Communications Company

*Printed in the United States of America*
*First printing: May 1988*
*10 9 8 7 6 5 4 3*
*Book design by Nick Mazzella*

**Library of Congress Cataloging-in-Publication Data**

Weller, Tom.
    The book of stupid questions / Tom Weller.
        p.   cm.
    ISBN 0-446-38972-2. (pbk) (USA) ISBN 0-446-38973-0 (pbk.) (Canada)
    1. Civilization—Anecdotes, facetiae, satire, etc.   2. Questions
and answers.   I. Title.
PN6231.C46W44 1988                                         87-37135
818'.5402—dc19                                              CIP

*To Socrates,*
*the first man to discover the hazards*
*of asking too many questions.*

# Introduction

This is not a book of trivia questions. Nor does it contain questions dealing with scientific, historical, or artistic fact; in no way do any of these questions impinge on the real world. What then is the point of this book? Ah, already we see how good questions lead to more questions!

No, these are questions about *you*—your fears, your hopes, your peculiar readiness to shell out good money for sophomoric pap. There are no "right" or "wrong" answers to these questions. Rather, they illustrate the old adage, "ask a stupid question, get a stupid answer."

You will be surprised how fast these questions can penetrate the superficial veneer of most daily conversation, and expose the real veneer beneath. A dull evening with some acquaintances turned into an exciting debate involving considerable damage to the furniture. An old friend with whom I fell to chatting one day hasn't returned my calls since. A casual encounter with a woman in a bus terminal led to a long, unpleasant scene involving the police.

The questions here deal with a variety of topics, ranging from the merely ridiculous to the truly pointless. Notice that they are arranged in random order, so that any faint hope of coherent thought is obviated. Notice, too, that this book consists mostly of blank paper. Use it as a tool. Take an active role in dealing with the questions, expanding them, changing the conditions, doodling on the pages, filling in all the "o"s. In short, don't think of this as just another book; think of it as a $3.95 pad of scratch paper.

As you explore your responses and challenge your value system, you may find that questioning has gone beyond being just an entertaining pastime, to being a real waste of time. So ask your friends. Ask your parents. Ask someone you hardly know. But please—don't ask me.

# THE
# BOOK OF
# STUPID
# QUESTIONS

# 1

If your mother-in-law and a lawyer were drowning, and you could only save one of them, would you have lunch or go to a movie?

# 2

If you found $1,000,000 in a wallet on the sidewalk, would you spend your summers in Greece or Puerto Vallarta?

# 3

Would you rather think you were smart but really be dumb or really be smart and think you were dumb?

# 4

What do you value most in a relationship: having someone to put a finger on the knot when wrapping a package or being able to order the "giant confusion" pizza?

# 5

Have you ever had an out-of-body experience? How about an out-of-mind experience?

# 6

Have you ever gone to first base? Second base? Third base? Home plate? Pop flyed out? Walked? Bunted to the pitcher? Been sent to the showers? Called on account of rain?

# 7

If you could redraw the boundaries of the state you live in, what shape would it be?

# 8

If you knew that by pondering ridiculously artificial pseudo-philosophical questions you could avoid dealing with real-world decisions, would you do it?

# 9

If you could choose between the body of a 20-year-old and the body of a 50-year-old, where would you keep it?

# 10

You are invited to a lavish party that is filled with glamorous, exciting, famous people. Why do you suppose they invited you?

# 11

Would you accept reincarnation if you knew you would come back as Phil Rizzuto of the Money Store?

# 12

You are driving on a steep mountain road when a dog suddenly darts in front of your car. There's no time to brake, and if you swerve to miss it, you will plunge off a steep cliff. What would you use to clean the blood off your chrome?

# 13

If you knew that you were going to die in one week, would you be able to max out your credit cards in that time?

Would you rather be completely penniless and look like Paul McCartney did in 1964 or be a millionaire and look like Paul McCartney does now?

# 15

If you had to eat one crayon out of a box of 64, which color would it be?

# 16

Which of these is the most important to you in your life: spiritual enlightement, good grooming, sex, pizza, electrical appliances, spray starch?

# 17

Would you rather be stupid or ugly?

# 18

Suppose that you answer the telephone and it's the President of the United States. He tells you that there is an intergalactic plague threatening both humans and a vastly superior race of gentle, wise beings. A vaccine exists, but there's only enough of the medicine to save one race. You have been selected at random to decide which one. So that your decision won't be prejudiced, your life will be spared, along with a few hundred fellow humans you select. Would you get your hearing checked?

# 19

Would you rather drink a Drano margarita or share a sleeping bag with a 200-pound tarantula?

# 20

If you were certain that by having your lips removed you could end the clubbing of baby harp seals, would you consider getting professional help?

# 21

What would constitute a "perfect" bowel movement for you?

# 22

If you were offered \$1,000,000 to move to a location so distant that you would probably never see your in-laws again, would you write at Christmas?

# 23

Would you rather slide down a razor blade into a barrel of iodine or drink a bucket of monkey snot?

# 24

Would you add a year to your life if it meant taking a year away from the life of some other person? Ok, what if the other person was Geraldo Rivera?

# 25

Do you always read the instructions before making a call from a pay phone?

# 26

When making important decisions, on which of the following do you usually rely: your horoscope, the *I Ching*, "voices" in your head, crystal gazing, or paperback self-help books?

# 27

Would you rather fall into a pit of tumescent baboons or spend two weeks stranded in Bozeman, Montana?

# 28

How annoyed would you be if some total stranger insisted on asking you a series of ridiculous, personal questions? Would it be just as bad if it was a friend at a party? A relative?

Assume you have a thousand dollars. Do you keep it, or go for what's behind curtain number three?

# 30

You suddenly become telepathic, and can see through the eyes of others and enter into their most private thoughts and desires. What is the best way of making a lot of money out of this?

# 31

What is your favorite internal organ?

If you suddenly found out that you have been inadvertently underpaying your taxes every year for your whole life, would you notify the Internal Revenue Service and demand that you be allowed to shoulder your fair share of the nation's debt, knowing that a clean conscience would be your only reward? Do you expect me to believe that?

# 33

What has been the biggest disappointment in your life, other than buying this book?

# 34

You and an attractive member of the opposite sex are trapped in an elevator. You are getting to know each other and the time is passing pleasantly when you become aware that you have to go to the bathroom really bad. What kind of arrangements do you make? Be specific.

# 35

If you could pick the exact day of your death, would it be a weekday or a holiday?

# 36

You are on a Greyhound bus traveling across rural Texas at the height of summer. An attractive stranger sits down next to you and you fall into a pleasant, witty conversation. Unexpectedly, the person offers you $10,000 to go back to the restroom and have sex. Would you accept a third-party check? How about out of state?

# 37

When, if ever, did you last change your socks?

# 38

If you had to have one of your ears surgically removed in order to save the world from certain nuclear holocaust, which ear would you choose?

# 39

Where does lint come from, and would you want to go there on a vacation?

# 40

If you could prevent either the entire continent of Asia from sinking into the sea, a mild outbreak of food poisoning at the Kiwanis Pancake Breakfast in your town, or you getting a paper cut on your tongue, which would you choose?

# 41

Did people pass around lists of fatuous questions like this when you were in 6th grade?

# 42

Have you ever seen a flying saucer? Have you ever been attacked by an aquatic rabbit? Have you ever committed adultery in your heart?

# 43

Would you rather be roasted alive over mesquite charcoal or be force-fed tofu until you burst?

# 44

Would you rather have a red hot poker up your nose or a charley horse on the bottom of your foot forever?

# 45

Do you ever lie? And why should I believe you?

# 46

Is it worse when you try to go up a step that's not there and hit thin air or when you try to go down a step that's not there and hit the floor?

# 47

Have you ever French kissed your dog?

# 48

Dining at a friend's house, you find a dead rat in your Jello. Which fork should you use?

# 49

If you discovered that you had been mixed up at the hospital as a baby, would you turn yourself in?

# 50

Would you be willing to move to a distant country and never return home if you knew that people there would consider your accent "cute"?

# 51

If God appeared to you in a dream and told you to take accordion lessons, would you do it?

# 52

If you were offered $1,000,000 on the condition that you leave your spouse (or mate) never to meet again, who would get the record collection?

# 53

Would you become a famous and wealthy doctor if your specialty had to be proctology?

# 54

After a medical examination, your doctor informs you that you have only six months to live. But you can't pay your bill, so he gives you another six months. Haven't you heard this joke before?

# 55

What breakfast cereal has had the greatest influence on your life?

Assume you are a writer. Would you write a fatuous and trashy "non-book" in return for $100,000 in royalties? Assume you are a publisher, and know that this worthless nonsense will be successful. Would you publish it?

# 57

If you had to have every disease in the world successively, in what order would you have them?

# 58

Would you be willing to restore a puppy to life by having a boil on the bottom of your foot? What about a rat? Who are you to judge the relative values of the earth's creatures? It's because one is furry and one is hairy, isn't it?

# 59

If a tree falls in the forest, and there's nobody there to hear it, who cares?

# 60

When having dinner at someone's house, do you ever refrain from jumping on the table and exposing yourself merely to avoid being thrown out?

# 61

Are you easily pressured into things by other people? Come on, answer up—and make it snappy!

# 62

Have you ever been taking a shower when—for no particular reason—you think of an old friend you haven't thought
of in years, and the doorbell rings, and when you get out
of the shower to answer it, it's the Jehovah's Witnesses?

# 63

If you could change the order of the alphabet, what order would you put the letters in?

# 64

Would it disturb you if, after death, your body were used as a set decoration on *Pee-wee's Playhouse*?

# 65

If you could live anywhere in the world, would you?

# 66

If you could take only one TV set with you to a desert island, what brand would it be?

# 67

How old were you when you had your first hangnail?

# 68

If you could save an innocent man from the gas chamber by falsely convicting a really bad person of a crime he didn't commit, would you do it? Well, who do you think you are, anyway? God?

# 69

Would you be willing to go to Hell if you got the Gatorade concession?

# 70

If you were offered a small book that, for only a few dollars, promised effortless enlightenment, spiritual growth, and self-improvement, would you fall for it again?

# 71

Would you eliminate all evil in the world if you knew that things would be pretty dull afterward? How about just some of it?

# 72

Would you be willing to personally cut off Bambi's legs with a chainsaw if it meant that there would never be another used car lot in the world?

# 73

If you were to die right now, what would happen to your laundry at the cleaners?

# 74

Would you eat worms if somebody gave you a quarter?
How about a dollar? Wouldja? Huh? Huh? Wouldja? Double
dare ya! Double dare ya!

How many angels can breakdance on the head of a pin?

# 76

You and a close friend are trapped in a mine cave-in. There is enough air in the mine shaft to keep one person alive for ten hours or two people alive for five hours—provided neither of them plays the harmonica. Also in the mine are a .45 revolver, a harmonica, and sheet music to "Gentle on My Mind." You can hear the rescue team coming closer. They yell through a small opening that they will be able to reach you in seven hours, or five hours if someone keeps their spirits up by playing "Gentle on My Mind" on the harmonica. Would you shoot (a) your friend, (b) the harmonica, (c) yourself, or (d) Glenn Campbell?

# 77

Have you ever been a member of an organization that advocated the overthrow of the United States government by force or violence?

# 78

Would you take an all-expense-paid trip around the world if it were non-stop?

# 79

Do you ever talk to yourself? If so, do you ever answer?

# 80

You go to the restroom in the middle of a really important date with the most fabulous person you've ever met. There you notice a big zit right on the end of your nose. Do you pop it right then or wait till you get home?

# 81

Have you ever wished you were a member of the opposite sex? And how do you know you're not?

# 82

You are in a lifeboat with a rabbi, a minister, and a priest. There are only three parachutes, and the air is giving out. In your pocket, you discover a half-eaten candy bar, a map of Columbus, Ohio, and an Uzi machine gun. What was the conductor's name?

# 83

If you could be an electrical appliance, would you rather be AC or DC?

# 84

You and your best friend are exploring a remote jungle. One day you are captured by an unknown tribe of natives, who take you to their princess, a beautiful blonde. You fall madly in love with her. Meanwhile your friend builds a dirigible from vines and bamboo. You escape and, after many adventures involving prehistoric beasts and giant gorillas, manage to reach civilization. Should the jungle princess get a percentage of the screen rights? What about points? Assuming you have casting approval, who do you see as the princess?

# 85

Would you dance naked in Macy's front window to save the whales? What about the snail darter? Is it because whales are bigger?

# 86

If you could learn the secret of the universe, but then immediately have all memory of it erased from your mind, it would be pretty pointless, wouldn't it?

# 87

Would you rather be staked out nude on an anthill or be forced to watch a Richard Chamberlain film festival?

# 88

A person you know to be greedy and rapacious in his personal dealings mistakenly gives you a $1000 bill thinking that he gave you a ten. Do you give him change for a ten and donate the balance to charity? Sure, you do.

# 89

Would you be willing to have your fingernails pulled out if you knew that it meant that John Cougar Mellencamp would never make another record?

# 90

Would you rather engage in earnest psychobabble passing for "learning about yourself" or watch reruns of *Gilligan's Island*?

How much would you charge to haunt a house?

# 92

If you had to choose between two bottles, one that contained a pill that 50% of the time increased your intelligence but made your nose fall off, and 50% of the time cured warts but made your fingernails turn black, and the other that had a 10% chance of turning you blind and deaf but the rest of the time brought world peace, or having your best friend thrown into a pit of . . . wait, I've lost track of the question.

# 93

Would you rather be extremely happy between the hours of 7 A.M. and 7 P.M. and really miserable from 7 P.M. to 7 A.M., or would you rather be miserable from 7 A.M. to 7 P.M. and happy from 7 P.M. to 7 A.M.?

Assume you are attending a black tie dinner at Henry Kissinger's. Could you refrain from leaping on the table and mooning the guests, if it meant stopping one of the doctor's monologues on the proper use of power in the twentieth century?

# 95

Is the sky really blue, or does it just look like it?

# 96

You buy a lottery ticket to give a friend for his birthday. You forget all about it until after the drawing, whereupon it turns out to be worth $42,000,000. Do you give your friend something of equivalent worth to make up for it—say, a framed portrait of yourself?

# 97

If you could choose, would you rather be yourself or some-one else just like you?

# 98

You buy a new house. While doing some remodeling you discover a buried pirate treasure under the floor. Do you break all speed records making sure that the former owner hears about what he or she missed? Do you gloat in a fake commiserating sort of way?

# 99

Do you have a favorite toe?

# 100

If you could save a million starving children by sacrificing one of the major TV networks, would you choose ABC, CBS, or NBC?

Had enough yet?

# 102

If you could choose from anyone in the world, who would you want as your tax preparer? Endodontist? Roto-Rooter man?

# 103

Where were you on the night of November 15, 1977?

# 104

If a new drug were discovered that prevented all diseases but made everyone that took it look like Wayne Newton, would you buy stock in Vaseline?

# 105

What is the capital of Mars?

# 106

If you could be painlessly turned into a cheerful, not-too-bright vegetable, would it change your lifestyle? Would you notice?

# 107

Which could you best tolerate: living on nothing but "Beer Nuts" for the rest of your life or having a picture of Robin Leach tattooed on your forehead?

# 108

You are having dinner with a date at a fancy restaurant. Suddenly a man runs in and shouts that the dead are rising from their graves and stalking the land, devouring the living. Everyone gets up to flee. Do you leave a tip?

# 109

Would you rather be extremely happy but not know it or be miserable but not care?

# 110

If you could pass your time with foolish daydreaming instead of doing a decent job of what you're supposed to be doing, would you endlessly mull over simple-minded questions like these?

Do you ever make faces at blind people?

# 112

Where does your lap go when you stand up?

# 113

Would you be willing to write a cruel parody of a sincere, heartfelt book that had brought comfort and innocent pleasure to millions, just to make a lot of money?

# Answers

Of course, there are no "right" or "wrong" answers to these questions. Every individual will have his own answer, meaningful only in terms of his or her personal experience. However, if you're stumped, a list of answers is supplied here. These answers do not correspond to any particular question; pick your answer at random, or glue this list to your Ouija board.

Yes

No

Yes, sir!

No, thank you

Maybe

1492

Seven

All of the above

The Wars of the Roses

98.6° F.

Trigger

Ask your father

Babe Ruth

Only when I laugh

No opinion

John, Paul, George, and Ringo

Ask again

Indianapolis

The New York Yankees, in 1923

The doctor was his mother

We'll see

The sum of the squares of the other two sides

Could you repeat the question?

Agree strongly

Disagree strongly

I respectfully decline to answer on the grounds that
my answer might tend to incriminate me

R-o-l-a-i-d-s

*Wings* (1927), Charles "Buddy" Rogers, Richard Arlen,
Clara Bow

Because

Because I said so

Because it's there

Both lines are the same length

Not at this address

I have no recollection of that at this time, Senator

4.2 light-years

A boojum, you see